Felix Mendelssohn

CHAMBER WORKS
FOR PIANO AND STRINGS

EDITED BY JULIUS RIETZ

From the Breitkopf & Härtel Complete Works Edition

DOVER PUBLICATIONS, INC.
New York

Published in Canada by General Publishing Company, Ltd.,
30 Lesmill Road, Don Mills, Toronto, Ontario.
Published in the United Kingdom by Constable and Company, Ltd.,
10 Orange Street, London WC2H 7EG.

This Dover edition, first published in 1989, is an
unabridged republication of *Serie 9. Für Pianoforte und Saiten-
instrumente* from *Felix Mendelssohn Bartholdy's Werke. Kritisch
durchgesehene Ausgabe von Julius Rietz. Mit Genehmigung der
Originalverleger* (original edition published 1874–1877).

Manufactured in the United States of America
Dover Publications, Inc.
31 East 2nd Street
Mineola, N.Y. 11501

Library of Congress Cataloging-in-Publication Data

Mendelssohn-Bartholdy, Felix, 1809–1847.
[Chamber music. Selections]
Chamber works for piano and strings.

Reprint. Originally published: Leipzig : Breitkopf & Härtel, ca. 1875 (Felix
Mendelssohn Bartholdy's Werke. Kritisch durchgesehene Ausgabe. Serie 9).
Contents: Sextet in D major for violin, 2 violas, cello, bass, and piano, op. 110
(1824) — Piano quartet no. 1 in C minor, op. 1 (1822) — Piano quartet no. 2 in F
minor, op. 2 (1823) — [etc.]
1. Sextets (Piano, violin, violas (2), violoncello, double bass)—Scores. 2. Piano
quartets—Scores. 3. Piano trios—Scores. 4. Sonatas (Violin and piano)—Scores.
5. Violoncello and piano music—Scores. I. Rietz, Julius, 1812–1877.
M178.M4R52   1989   89-752451
ISBN 0-486-26117-4 (pbk.)

CONTENTS

Sextet in D Major for Violin, 2 Violas, Cello, Bass, and Piano, Op. 110

Adagio.

Adagio.

Menuetto D.C.

Allegro con fuoco.

Allegro con fuoco.

Piano Quartet No. 1
in C Minor, Op. 1

Scherzo D.C. al Fine.

Piano Quartet No. 2
in F Minor, Op. 2

Intermezzo.
Allegro moderato.

Piano Quartet No. 3
in B Minor, Op. 3

Piano Trio No. 1
in D Minor, Op. 49

SCHERZO.

Leggiero e vivace.

Finale.
Allegro assai appassionato.

Piano Trio No. 2
in C Minor, Op. 66

SCHERZO.

Molto Allegro quasi Presto. M. M. ♩=88.

FINALE.

Allegro appassionato. M.M. ♩.=112.

Violin Sonata
in F Minor, Op. 4

Allegro agitato.

Variations Concertantes
for Cello and Piano, Op. 17

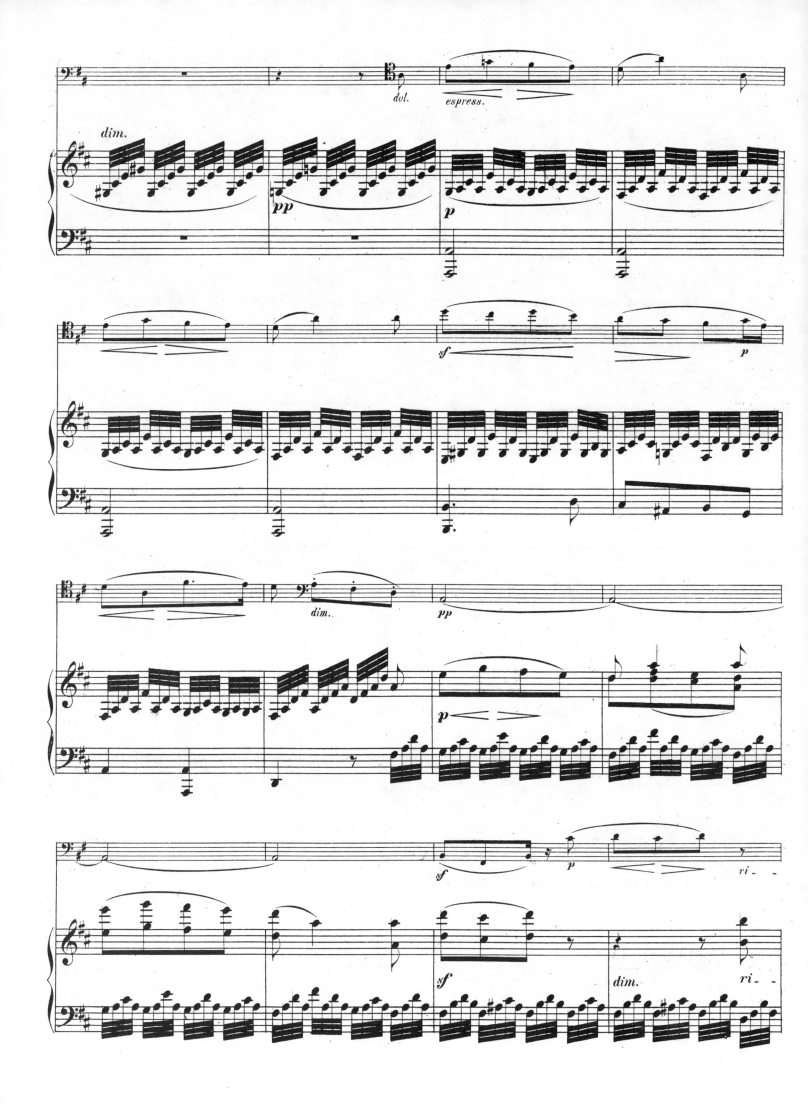

Cello Sonata No. 1
in B-flat Major, Op. 45

Cello Sonata No. 2
in D Major, Op. 58

Allegretto scherzando.

Molto Allegro e vivace.

Lied ohne Worte
for Cello and Piano, Op. 109